Empty Nest Recovery Journal

5-Minute Daily Prompts to Rediscover Yourself & Reimagine Life Beyond Motherhood

Amber D. Campbell

Empty Nest Recovery Journal:
5-Minute Daily Prompts to
Rediscover Yourself &
Reimagine Life Beyond Motherhood

Published by Blue Dawn Press
PO Box 18893, Seattle, WA 98118
Cover Design by Amber D. Campbell

ISBN: 979-8-9934997-2-7

"The art of mothering is to teach the art of living."

Elaine Hefner

Why this Journal?

When the kids are gone and the house grows quiet, so many emotions can rise to the surface — grief, pride, nostalgia, relief, even a bit of panic. After years of being needed every day, it can feel alternately weird and wonderful to finally have space for yourself again.

And that's where the magic starts.

Numerous research studies show that reflective journaling can help us think clearly and make better choices by reducing anxiety, sharpening our thinking, reducing mental clutter, and clarifying our values.

But beyond the data, journaling gives us something even more powerful: a place to meet ourselves honestly on the page, sort through the noise, and remember who we are beyond the expectations of others.

This journal will guide you through six gentle sections:

- Grieving & Grounding
- Releasing Roles & Expectations
- Rediscovering Your Identity
- Reimagining Relationships
- Reigniting Your Purpose
- Creating Your Next Chapter

Each section builds on the last, guiding you toward the answers already within you.

How to Use this Journal

As you embark on this journey, keep a few things in mind:

Be kind to yourself. This is your healing space. Write freely, without judgment, and allow yourself to be as messy and raw as you need to be.

Five minutes a day is enough. Each page offers a single prompt. Start with a deep breath and write whatever comes to mind.

Try anchoring your practice. Pick one daily practice such as morning coffee, teeth brushing, bedtime, whatever, and commit to writing before, after, or during.

There's no wrong way to do it. This journal is for you, and only you. Meeting yourself honestly on the page is more important than finding the perfect words.

Skip or return as needed. If a particular prompt feels too heavy one day, move on and pick another. You can always come back later.

Protect your privacy. Keep this journal somewhere safe, so you can feel free to write honestly. Consider purchasing an inexpensive lock box, if necessary.

1

Grieving & Grounding

What do you miss most about the time when your kids still lived at home?

What, if anything, feels like a relief right now?

How has the rhythm of your days changed since the nest emptied?

What emotions do you notice most often, and what might they be trying to tell you?

What are you learning about yourself in the quiet moments?

What parts of your identity feel most uncertain right now?

When you picture this next season, what fears come up?

"What is stronger than
the human heart which
shatters over and over
and still lives?"

Rupi Kaur

What does home mean to you now?

What gives you comfort when you feel lonely or adrift?

Write down one thing you're ready to forgive yourself for.

What helps you feel most grounded in your body and emotions?

How do you know when you're avoiding your feelings? How can you face them with compassion?

What do you want to remember about this transition in 10 years?

How has your sense of purpose shifted since your children became independent?

2
Releasing Roles & Expectations

Which expectations (your own or others') feel heaviest right now?

Where do you still try to control what's no longer yours to manage?

What stories about motherhood or womanhood no longer fit?

When do you feel the most the pressure to have it all together?

What parts of yourself have you postponed or hidden in service to others?

Write a permission slip to yourself for this new season.

How does it feel to imagine life where you're not needed all the time?

"With age, I am learning
to be braver, to show up
for myself with the same
devotion I once gave
everyone else."

Cheryl Strayed

Which external standards, such as beauty, success, or productivity, are you ready to release?

What would you do differently if you didn't care what others thought?

How does it feel to imagine being the main character in your own story again?

When were you last free of responsibility, and how did it feel?

Which beliefs about aging or midlife are you ready to rewrite?

What does it mean to mother yourself?

Who are you when no one needs anything from you?

3
Rediscovering Your Identity

What brings you joy that has nothing to do with anyone else?

How have you changed in the last five years? What do you like about those changes?

What values matter most to you in this stage of life?

What hobbies, passions, or curiosities have you set aside for too long?

Who were you before motherhood, and what parts are calling you back?

What are you naturally good at that you've never fully claimed?

What makes you feel beautiful and powerful?

"I am out with lanterns
looking for myself."

Emily Dickinson

What would your best friend say are your greatest gifts?

What compliments are hardest for you to accept? Why?

How do you want to describe yourself three years from now?

What lights you up so much that you lose track of time?

When do you feel most curious or creative?

What did you once love that you might love again?

What do you want to learn or try just for you?

4
Reimagining Relationships

How has your relationship with your children evolved?

What do you appreciate about them as adults?

What boundaries help you stay close without losing yourself?

How can you offer support without overstepping?

What kind of intimacy or connection do you crave now?

How are friendships shifting in this stage of life?

Who truly sees and celebrates you as you are?

"Give the ones you
love wings to fly,
roots to come back
and reasons to stay."

The Dalai Lama

What are some ways you can deepen your relationship with yourself?

Who do you miss, and what keeps you from reaching out?

What do you want your adult children to learn from watching you now?

How do you want to be loved in this season of life?

What kind of community or sisterhood do you want to build?

How can you practice vulnerability with the people who matter most?

What does it look like to be your own best friend?

5
Reigniting Your Purpose

What makes you feel most alive?

What impact do you still want to make in the world?

What would you do if you knew it was impossible to fail?

What kind of legacy do you want to leave?

What dreams have been whispering at the edges of your awareness?

What causes, ideas, or passions tug at your heart?

When do you feel most useful or fulfilled?

"It's never too late
for a new beginning."

Charmaine J. Forde

What part of your story might inspire someone else?

What's one thing you've always wanted to learn, build, or create?

What are you curious about lately?

How might you combine your skills, passions, and experience in a new way?

Who or what inspires you to be brave?

What would a joyful, purposeful day look like to you?

How does it feel when you imagine putting your energy into something just for you?

6
Creating Your Next Chapter

What do you want more of, and less of, in your life?

What boundaries or routines will help protect your peace?

List three things you're grateful for this week.

What are you ready to say yes to?

What are you finally ready to say no to?

What's one bold dream that still scares you a little?

What do you want your 70-year-old self to thank you for?

"The future belongs to
those who believe in the
beauty of their dreams."

Eleanor Roosevelt

What does home look and feel like in this season?

Who do you want alongside you for this next adventure?

How can you celebrate yourself more often?

What possibilities excite you the most about midlife?

How will you keep growing — creatively, emotionally, spiritually?

What rituals or practices help you stay connected to your joy?

If nothing were holding you back, what would you do next?

7
Reflections

Looking back on your journey, what's changed in how you see yourself, your future, and your freedom?

What hopes, dreams, and intentions will you carry forward into your next chapter?

"To live in this world you must
be able to do three things:
to love what is mortal; to hold
it against your bones knowing
your own life depends on it;
and, when the time comes to
let it go, to let it go."

Mary Oliver

About the Author

Amber D. Campbell is a writer and midlife coach dedicated to helping women heal, rebuild, and rediscover themselves after major life transitions.

When her own kids flew the nest, Amber felt like she'd been laid off from the most important job she'd ever done. Then she realized what a wonderful opportunity it was to rediscover herself and reimagine life beyond motherhood.

With a background in Family Studies and years of personal growth, Amber turned her own hard-won lessons into her mission: helping other women navigate midlife transitions like empty nest, divorce, career change, and parenting grownish kids with humor, grace, and strength.

When she's not writing or coaching, Amber can be found reading, traveling, or exploring nature, always with a strong cup of coffee nearby.

Also by Amber D. Campbell

The Midlife Magic Journal Series:

- *Divorce Recovery Journal: 5-Minute Daily Prompts to Heal After High-Conflict Divorce & Free Yourself from a Toxic Ex*
- *Family Estrangement Recovery Journal: 5-Minute Daily Prompts to Release the Shame & Free Yourself from a Toxic Family*

Learn more at midlifemagicwithamber.com

MIDLIFE MAGIC WITH AMBER
JUST WRITE ABOUT IT!

Scan now to join
the Midlife Magic
community!

Made in the USA
Coppell, TX
21 April 2026

75858462R10069